The · Life Cycle · Series

The Life Cycle of a

MOSQUITO

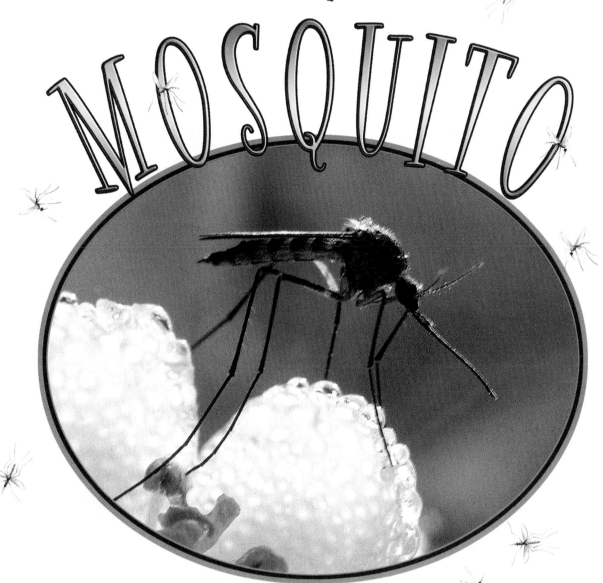

Bobbie Kalman

Crabtree Publishing Company

www.crabtreebooks.com

The Life Cycle Series

A Bobbie Kalman Book

Dedicated by Crystal Foxton
To my brother Kevin, for being the loving "pest" that he is!

Author and Editor-in-Chief
Bobbie Kalman

Research
Hadley Dyer

Substantive editor
Amanda Bishop

Editors
Molly Aloian
Kelley MacAulay
Rebecca Sjonger
Kathryn Smithyman

Art director
Robert MacGregor

Design
Margaret Amy Reiach

Production coordinator
Heather Fitzpatrick

Photo research
Crystal Foxton

Consultant
Patricia Loesche, Ph.D., Animal Behavior Program,
Department of Psychology, University of Washington

Special thanks to
Centers for Disease Control and Prevention (CDC)

Photographs
© CDC: page 10; James Gathany: front cover (mosquito), pages 12, 18, 20,
   27 (bottom), 29; Graham Heid and Dr. Harry D. Pratt: pages 26, 30 (top);
   W.H.O.: page 8
Bruce Coleman Inc.: Kim Taylor: pages 13 (top), 30 (bottom)
© Dwight R. Kuhn: pages 4, 13 (bottom), 14, 15, 16, 21 (top), 23, 28, 31
Robert McCaw: title page, pages 3, 5 (bottom), 21 (bottom), 25
Minden Pictures: Jim Brandenburg: page 17; Michio Hoshino: page 19
Visuals Unlimited: Bill Beatty: page 24; Dr. Dennis Kunkel: page 11;
   Kjell Sandved: page 5 (top); Science VU: page 27 (top)
Other images by Digital Vision

Illustrations
Barbara Bedell: page 27
Katherine Kantor: front and back cover, border, title page, pages 4, 5, 6, 7,
   9, 19, 20, 21, 22, 24, 26, 28, 29, 30, 31

Digital prepress
Embassy Graphics

Printer
Worzalla Publishing Company

Crabtree Publishing Company

www.crabtreebooks.com   1-800-387-7650

PMB 16A	612 Welland Avenue	73 Lime Walk
350 Fifth Avenue	St. Catharines	Headington
Suite 3308	Ontario	Oxford
New York, NY	Canada	OX3 7AD
10118	L2M 5V6	United Kingdom

Cataloging-in-Publication Data
Kalman, Bobbie.
   The life cycle of a mosquito / Bobbie Kalman.
      p. cm. -- (The life cycle series)
   Includes index.
   ISBN 0-7787-0665-6 (RLB) -- ISBN 0-7787-0695-8 (pbk.)
   1. Mosquitoes--Life cycles--Juvenile literature. [1. Mosquitoes.]
I. Title.
   QL536.K35 2004
   595.77'2--dc22
                                                    2003027692
                                                    LC

Contents

What is a mosquito?

A mosquito is a tiny flying **insect**. Insects are **invertebrates**, or animals that do not have backbones. Like all insects, every mosquito has six legs and a pair of wings. There are more than 3,000 **species**, or types, of mosquitoes. They live all over the world. About 200 mosquito species live in North America.

Tough stuff

Mosquitoes are best known for their buzz and for their bite, but there is much more to learn about these amazing animals. They have lived on Earth since the time of the dinosaurs! In order to survive, mosquitoes have **adapted**, or become suited, to changes in their environment.

*This mosquito was trapped in **amber**, or sap from an ancient tree, about 38 million years ago!*

So many mosquitoes!

Mosquitoes are found all over the world. They almost always live near water. Many mosquito species live in places that are warm, shady, and damp, such as swamps, forests, and jungles. Mosquitoes can also be found in parks, on farms, in cities, and in your back yard! A few species live in very cold places, such as the Arctic, but they are active only during the warm summer months. Some species also live in deserts, but they are active only when it rains.

During the short summers in northern regions, animals such as this deer are often covered with biting mosquitoes!

Mosquitoes up close

Every mosquito's body has three main parts. The head holds all the **sensory organs**, or parts that sense light, sound, heat, and odor. The **thorax** is the middle section of the body. The wings and legs are attached to the thorax.

The **abdomen** is where **digestion**, or the breakdown of food, occurs. The diagrams below show some of the differences between male and female mosquitoes.

The common house mosquito is ⅛ to ¼ of an inch (0.3-0.6 cm) long.

A female mosquito

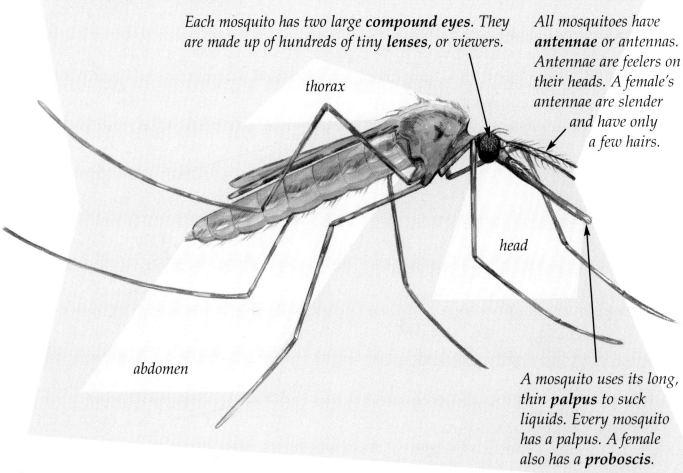

*Each mosquito has two large **compound eyes**. They are made up of hundreds of tiny **lenses**, or viewers.*

*All mosquitoes have **antennae** or antennas. Antennae are feelers on their heads. A female's antennae are slender and have only a few hairs.*

thorax

head

abdomen

*A mosquito uses its long, thin **palpus** to suck liquids. Every mosquito has a palpus. A female also has a **proboscis**.*

Mosquito relatives

Mosquitoes belong to a group of insects called true flies. A true fly has one pair of wings, a small body, and a mouth with sucking parts. Crane flies, midges, and gnats are also true flies.

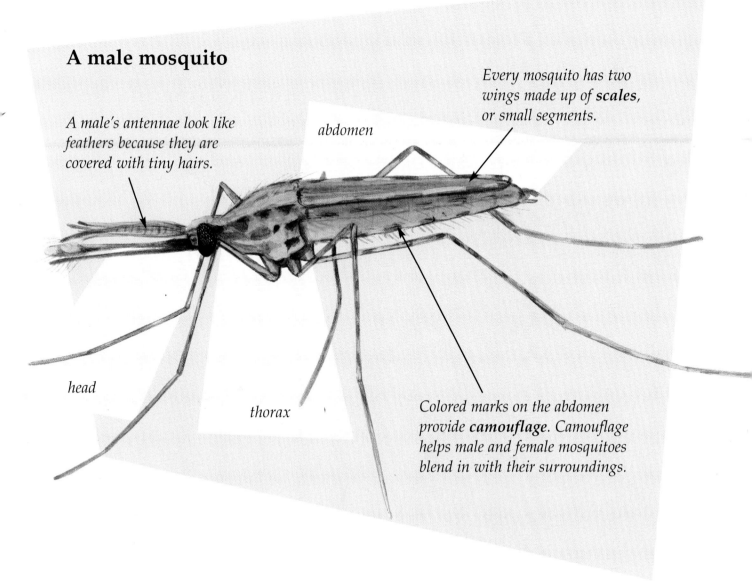

A male mosquito

A male's antennae look like feathers because they are covered with tiny hairs.

*Every mosquito has two wings made up of **scales**, or small segments.*

abdomen

head

thorax

*Colored marks on the abdomen provide **camouflage**. Camouflage helps male and female mosquitoes blend in with their surroundings.*

What is a life cycle?

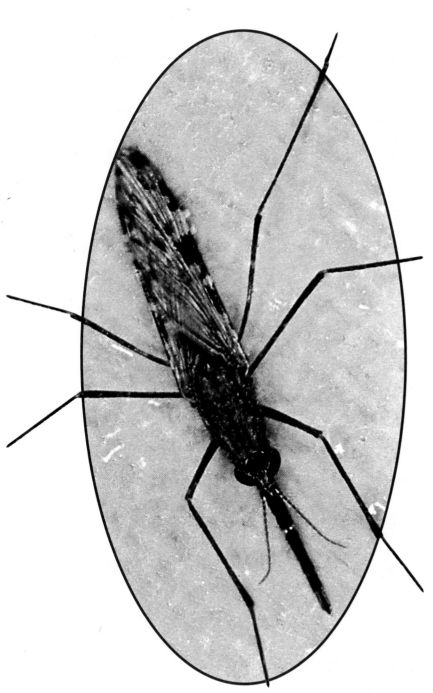

Every animal goes through a set of **stages**, or changes, called a **life cycle**. First, it is born or hatches from an egg. The animal then grows and changes until it becomes an adult. As an adult, a mosquito can **reproduce**, or make babies. All mosquitoes go through these stages during their life cycles.

Life span

An animal's life cycle is not the same as its **life span**. A life span is the length of time an animal is alive. Mosquitoes can live as long as five or six months, but few survive that long. Most live less than three weeks.

A mosquito's life cycle

A mosquito begins its life inside an egg. A baby mosquito, called a **larva**, hatches from the egg. As the larva grows, its **cuticle**, or skin, becomes tight. The larva then **molts**, or sheds, its cuticle. When the larva is fully grown, it molts for the last time. The larva is now a **pupa**. Its body changes completely during this stage. The set of changes that take place in its body is called **metamorphosis**. Once its body is finished changing, the pupa's cuticle splits open. An **imago**, or new mosquito, **emerges**, or crawls out. It will soon be **mature**. Mature mosquitoes are able to **mate**, or join together to make babies. After a female has mated, she lays her eggs. A new life cycle begins with each egg.

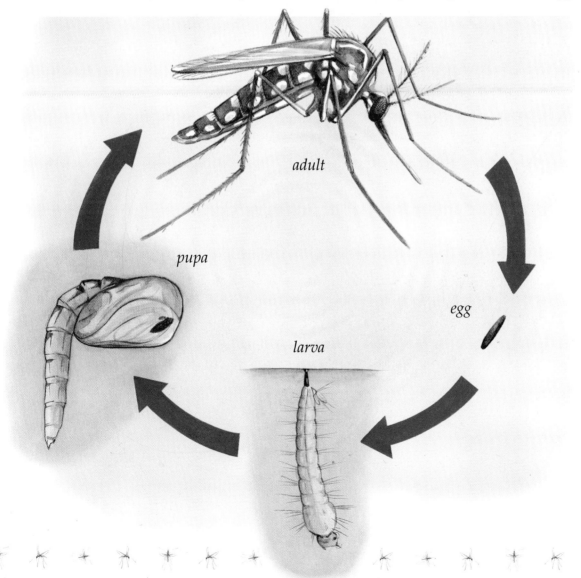

adult

pupa

egg

larva

Inside the egg

Every mosquito begins its life cycle inside an egg. Most mosquito eggs are laid in water. Some mosquito species lay their eggs in places that will soon be **immersed**, or covered by water, such as dips where puddles form. The eggs look like tiny seeds as they float on the water. They stay afloat on air bubbles at the water's surface.

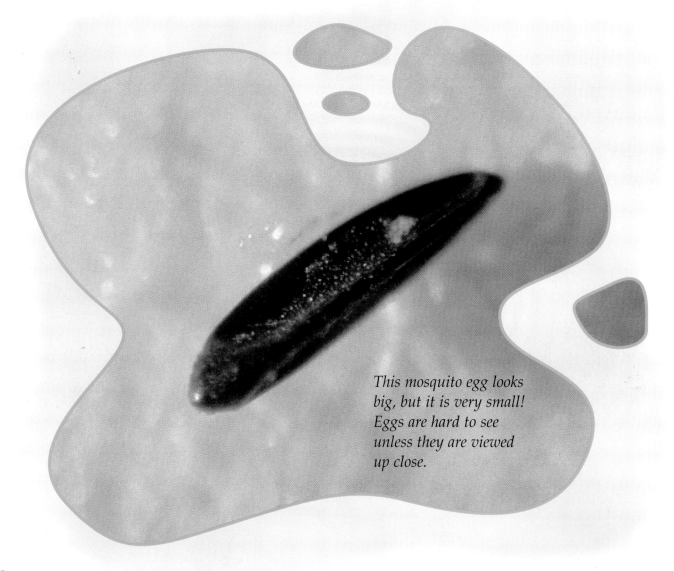

This mosquito egg looks big, but it is very small! Eggs are hard to see unless they are viewed up close.

Inside the egg

As soon as an egg has been laid, an **embryo**, or developing baby, starts growing inside. The embryo develops with its head pointing downward. The egg hatches after a few days. Most eggs that are laid at the same time also hatch at the same time. The **larvae**, or larvas, that emerge from the eggs then begin the next stage of their life cycles.

Tucked in tight

If the air outside grows cold, embryos may delay their development inside their eggs. Cold temperatures usually mean that winter is coming. When the temperature drops, the embryos become **dormant**, or inactive. A blanket of snow helps protect them from wind and ice. The embryos do not become active again until winter passes. When the weather warms up, they continue growing.

A special camera shows a close-up of a mosquito larva as it hatches from its egg.

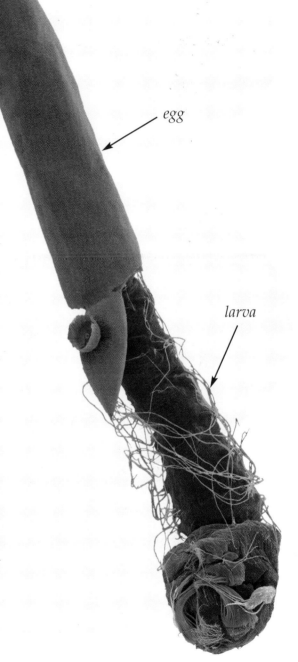

egg

larva

Little larvae

When a larva emerges from its egg, it swims downward one or two inches (2.5-5 cm) before bobbing up to the water's surface. The larva does not look like an adult! Its long, thin body is covered with hairs. The hairs help keep the larva steady in an up-and-down position in the water, as shown below. Hairs also help the larva sense movements around its body.

Larvae must breathe air in order to stay alive. Many species breathe by poking their tails out of the water. There are air tubes inside the tails. The larvae use the air tubes to breathe the air above the water's surface. A few species do not have air tubes. They must get air in other ways. Some attach their tails to plant stems and breathe from the air bubbles inside the plants.

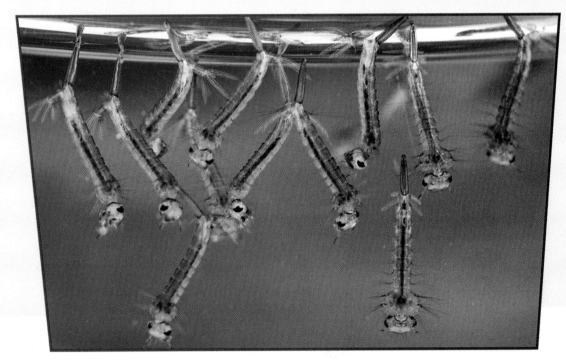

These larvae stay close to the water's surface in order to breathe the air above it.

Time to eat!

A larva must eat a lot in order to grow. To feed, the larva waves the **bristles**, or hairs, around its mouth. The bristles move through the water several times per second to sweep food toward the larva's mouth. Larvae eat tiny plants and animals as well as other **particles**, or pieces, of food floating in the water.

Larvae and pupae of some species may attach their bodies to the stem of an underwater plant in order to get air.

A new skin

The larva eats as much as it can to grow bigger. Its cuticle does not grow, however. When a larva becomes too big for its cuticle, it molts. A new cuticle is ready under the old one. Each larva molts a total of four times.

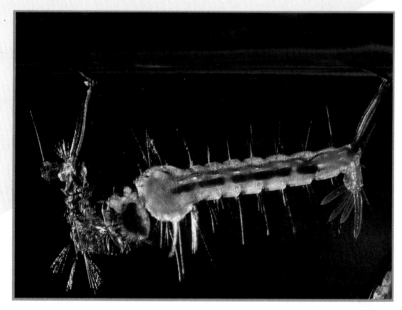

A larva eats the cuticle that another larva has shed.

A pupa transforms

When a mosquito larva molts for the last time, it becomes a pupa. The pupa's cuticle is soft at first, but it soon hardens. A mosquito goes through the biggest changes of its life while it is a pupa.

When the larva molts for the last time, a pupa emerges.

Curvy critters

The pupa does not look like a larva. Its body is now curved. Its head and thorax are joined to form a **cephalothorax**. The cephalothorax floats near the water's surface. Two **trumpets**, or breathing tubes, are attached to it. The pupa must rise regularly so that the trumpets poke above the water. The pupa can breathe air only when the trumpets break the water's surface.

The pupa has eyes on its cephalothorax, but it has no mouth. It does not eat during this stage of its life cycle.

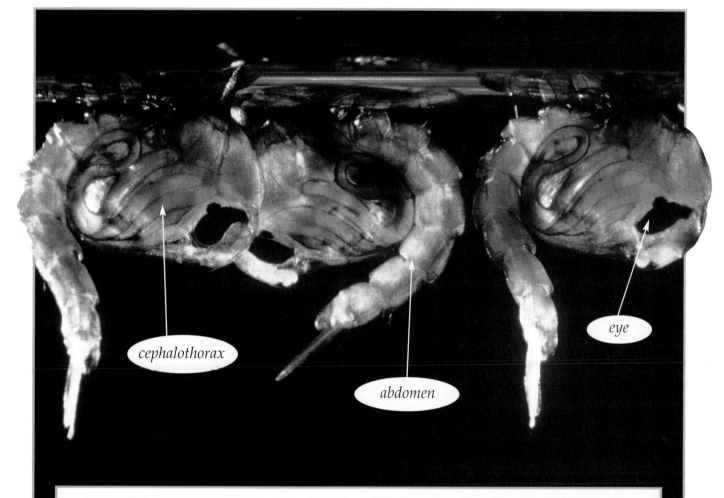

cephalothorax

abdomen

eye

Getting around

A pupa's large eyes detect movement above and below the water's surface. If the pupa senses movement nearby, it moves out of harm's way. The pupa "tumbles" down through the water by flicking its abdomen, which looks like a tail. The **segments**, or sections, of the abdomen are moveable. Special parts on the last segment help the pupa move through water.

What is going on in there?

Inside the cuticle, the pupa completes metamorphosis to become an adult mosquito. Its body parts **dissolve**, or break down. Adult parts such as an **exoskeleton**, wings, and **organs** form. When metamorphosis is finished, an imago has formed inside the pupa's cuticle. The pupa then stretches out below the water's surface. Its cuticle splits open, and the imago emerges.

An adult emerges

At first, the body of an imago is very soft. The imago must stay hidden until it has finished growing. It flies to a sheltered place as soon as it is able—usually about half an hour after it has emerged.

After another day or two, the imago has completely matured. During this last stage of its life cycle, the mosquito is no longer able to live underwater because it can no longer swim. Instead, it can fly!

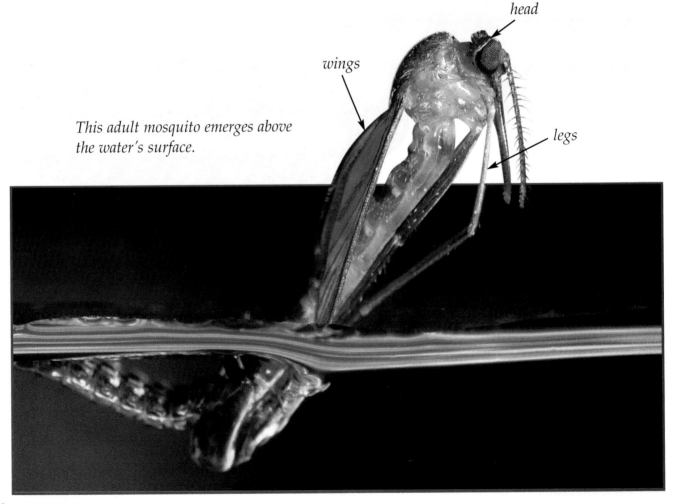

This adult mosquito emerges above the water's surface.

wings

head

legs

Sweet nectar

Before long, the adult is ready to look for its first meal. Male and female adult mosquitoes feed regularly on fruit juices and **nectar**, a sweet liquid made by flowers. Females of many species also need to eat a special meal—blood! See pages 20 to 21 for more information on why some mosquitoes need to drink blood.

Keeping warm

Adult mosquitoes are less active in cool weather. During the winter, some species **hibernate**. Mosquitoes often hibernate in sheltered places such as animal dens, hollow logs, and even the basements of buildings.

Ready to mate

By the time a mosquito is a few days old, it is ready to mate. Mating usually takes place at daybreak or at sunset. In some species, male mosquitoes form a gathering called a **swarm** near a **swarm marker** such as a building, a tree, or even an animal! When females find a swarm, they fly into it one by one. Their **wing beat**, or the sound of their beating wings, lets the males know they are female. Many males approach the same female, but only one mates with her. Mosquitoes mate by joining their abdomens. **Sperm** from the male's body then **fertilizes** the female's eggs, or causes babies to grow inside them. Females usually mate only once in their lives, but males mate as often as they can.

When mosquitoes are ready to mate, the male flies under the female and brings his abdomen up to meet hers.

Moving to the beat

A mosquito's buzz is the sound its wings make as they beat back and forth to fly. Depending on the species, a mosquito's wings beat 250 to 600 times per second! Male mosquitoes use their antennae to detect a female's wing beat. Males have been known to swarm machines that make noises similar to the wing beats of females!

Scientists are not sure why mosquitoes use certain objects as swarm markers. Big animals, such as this moose, may become swarm markers because their bodies give off heat.

Mosquito bites

After a female mosquito mates with a male, her eggs are fertilized. Some mosquito species need to eat a special meal before they can lay their eggs, however. As soon as a female from one of these species has mated, she sets off to find a **blood meal**. Animal blood contains the **nutrients**, or food energy, she needs for her eggs.

When the female finds an animal to bite, she lands on it. She uses two pairs of **stylets**, or cutting parts, to break the surface of the animal's skin. She then pushes her proboscis into the skin to find a **blood vessel**, or a tube through which blood moves.

This mosquito's abdomen stretches to make room for the blood she is drinking.

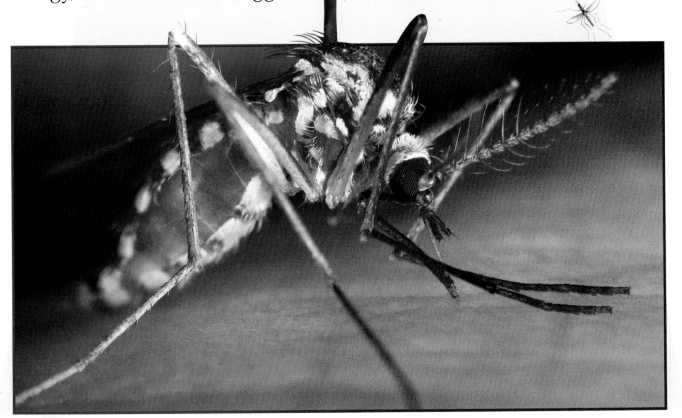

The probing proboscis

The proboscis has two tubes. The mosquito sucks up an animal's blood through one of the tubes. The mosquito's **saliva** enters the animal's blood vessel through the other tube. The saliva stops the animal's blood from **clotting**, or thickening. Blood that does not clot flows easily while the mosquito drinks as much as she needs.

proboscis

Most mosquitoes that drink blood meals bite birds, reptiles, or furry animals. There are only a few species that bite humans.

A full belly

It takes less than two minutes for a mosquito to fill her stomach with blood. A full stomach makes the mosquito's body heavy, so it is difficult for her to fly at first. When she is able, she flies to another surface on which to **digest** her meal. The mosquito then finds a safe place to rest for a few days. During this time, her eggs grow inside her body. She leaves her sheltered resting place to eat nectar only a few times.

Laying eggs

When a female is ready to lay her eggs, she finds a good place for laying. All species of mosquitoes lay their eggs in or near water because the eggs need to be covered with water when they hatch. Some species lay eggs on moist ground that is regularly covered by water. Most species, however, lay eggs on the surface of **standing water**, or water that is still. Ponds, marshes, pools, puddles, rain barrels, birdbaths, and clogged gutters are common places for mosquitoes to lay eggs.

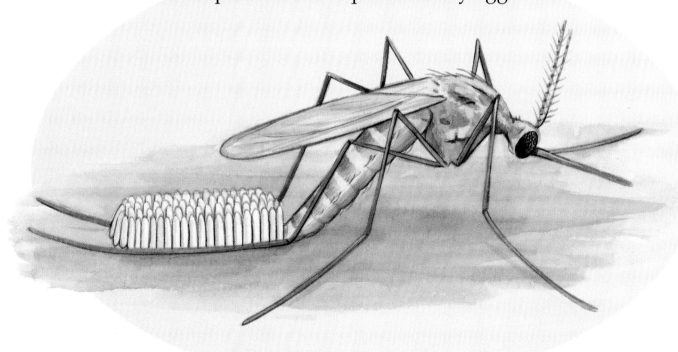

To lay eggs, a mosquito crosses her back legs and lowers her abdomen. She lays her eggs one by one. As each egg leaves her body, she twitches. The twitching turns the egg so the embryo inside will grow with its head pointing down.

Egg rafts

Females of some mosquito species lay their eggs one by one and set each egg afloat. Other species attach their eggs to plants. Many mosquito species create **egg rafts**. The rafts are made up of 100 to 300 eggs. To create a raft, a female holds the eggs between her legs as she lays them, as shown on page 22. Some species guard their egg rafts, but most set the rafts afloat and never see them again.

Once in a lifetime

Most females die shortly after they lay eggs for the first time. A female that survives longer, however, can lay more eggs. She may store some sperm in her body after mating. The sperm can then be used to fertilize more eggs. Before she lays the new eggs, a female must eat another blood meal.

Mosquito eggs are usually a light color at first, but they darken to black or brown within a day.

A dangerous life

Mosquitoes are faced with many dangers during their short lives. Many mosquitoes do not survive past the first or second stage of their life cycles. Eggs are often destroyed before they hatch. Larvae may not get enough food to eat while they are growing. Some larvae and **pupae**, or pupas, die if the natural conditions in which they live are spoiled. Larvae and pupae are also eaten by many **predators**, or animals that eat other animals for food. Their predators include fish, birds, tree frogs, snakes, and spiders.

*Mosquitoes at all stages of their life cycles may be eaten by **carnivorous**, or meat-eating, plants. This sundew has snared an adult mosquito.*

Danger everywhere!

Predators are a constant danger to mosquitoes. Mosquito fish feed on larvae underwater. Other predators, such as water striders, hunt from above. If a larva detects a water strider approaching, it wiggles down into the water to hide near the bottom—but it is not yet safe! Whirligig beetles, another type of predator, dive into the water to catch larvae that are making their way downward.

A meal of mosquitoes

Adult mosquitoes are a favorite meal of many animals. Ants often make a meal of mosquitoes that are resting after eating a blood meal. The nutrients in a blood-filled belly are attractive to predators. Bats are also excellent mosquito hunters. They use **echolocation**, or the ability to locate objects using sound, to find mosquitoes at night.

Mosquitoes are important members of many ***food chains***. *A food chain is made up of predators and their* ***prey***, *or animals that are hunted as food.*

25

Watch out!

Mosquitoes that bite humans can be dangerous if the mosquitoes carry **diseases**, or serious illnesses. Many diseases are caused by **parasites**, or animals that live inside the bodies of other animals. If a mosquito feeds on the blood of an animal that has a disease, the mosquito also drinks the parasites that live in the blood. The parasites do not make the mosquito sick, but the mosquito may become a parasite **carrier**. It passes the parasites into the blood of other animals that it bites. The parasites may then cause diseases.

These old tires collect water. They are good places for mosquitoes to lay eggs. If the mosquitoes that live here carry diseases, any people and animals living nearby may be in danger of getting sick.

Getting sick

Not all diseases can be carried by mosquitoes, but many are. Mosquitoes can spread malaria, yellow fever, dengue, encephalitis, and West Nile virus. Malaria, yellow fever, and dengue are most common in regions close to the equator. West Nile virus and a few types of encephalitis are found in North America. There are treatments, **vaccines**, and cures for some of these diseases, but many people and animals continue to suffer and even die from them.

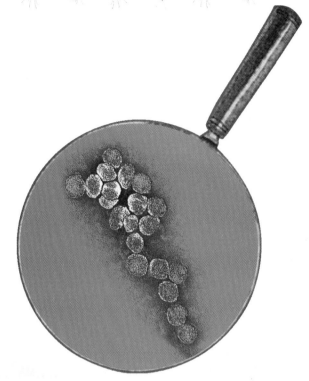

West Nile virus, shown here up close, is a growing threat to people in North America.

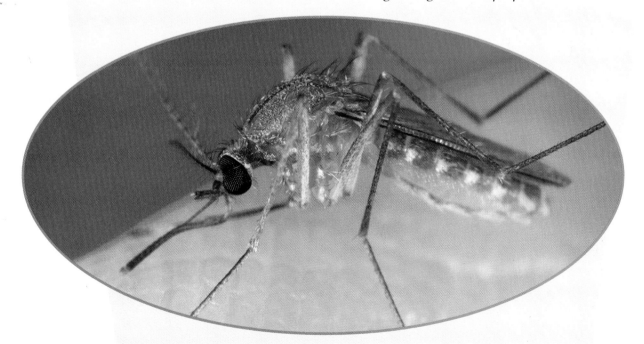

The southern house mosquito is one species known for carrying the West Nile virus. The virus is usually spread by mosquitoes that feed on infected birds and then bite humans.

How to stay safe

How do mosquitoes find their blood meals? How can you keep from being bitten? Mosquitoes use their senses to find blood meals. For example, did you know that movements such as swatting at mosquitoes make you an easy target? Mosquitoes smell a chemical called **lactic acid** that is produced by moving muscles.

Mosquitoes also smell **carbon dioxide**, a gas that is exhaled by animals when they breathe. The scent of this gas is heavier than air, so it sinks toward the ground. A mosquito flies low so it can catch these scents on its antennae. You cannot stop moving or breathing to avoid mosquito bites, but there are some things you can do!

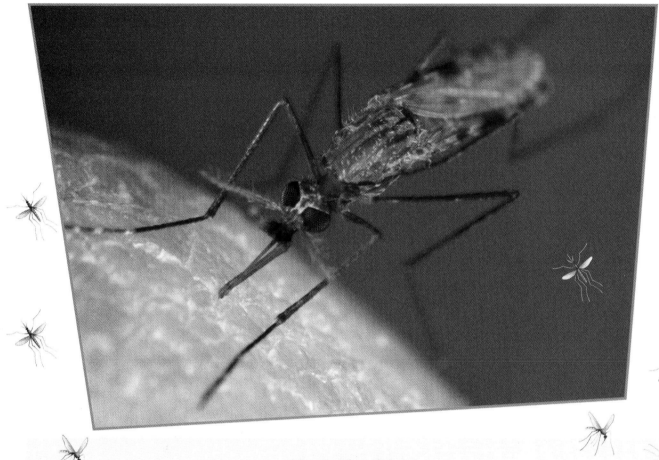

Beat the bite!

The following tips are important if you spend a lot of time outdoors.

- Be on the lookout for mosquitoes when you are outdoors.
- Mosquitoes see dark colors better than light colors. They also sense heat from your body. Wear light-colored clothing such as a hat, a long-sleeved shirt, and long pants. If your skin is covered, your body heat is harder to detect.
- Avoid spending time outdoors at sunrise and sunset, when many mosquitoes are most active.

- Ask an adult to help you apply an **insect repellent**. Wash off the repellent when you go indoors.
- If a mosquito bites you, wash the bite with soap and water. Place an ice pack on the bite. Ask an adult to apply calamine lotion or another anti-itch cream to help stop itching. Vinegar may also help take away the itch.
- Always remember to tell an adult if you have been bitten by a mosquito!

Learn more

Now that you know why mosquitoes bite and how to avoid getting bitten, you may want to find more fascinating facts about these incredible insects. Mosquitoes are some of the most interesting creatures on Earth, and there is a lot to learn about them!

*People can prevent mosquitoes from living near their homes without using dangerous **pesticides**, or chemicals that kill insects. Eliminate standing water, such as puddles, and change birdbath water every day.*

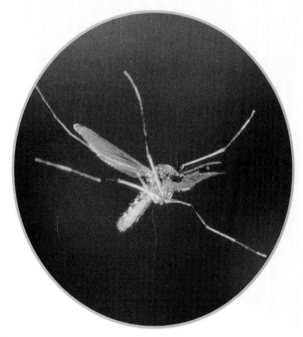

Staying safe

Scientists study mosquitoes to learn more about the way their bodies work and about the diseases they carry. They also come up with ways to prevent mosquitoes and humans from coming into close contact. Many towns and cities work hard to keep mosquitoes away from areas where a lot of people live. Find out how you can make your own house and yard safe from mosquitoes. Make sure your family, friends, and neighbors know, too!

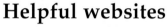

Helpful websites

If you want to discover more about the magnificent mosquito, try visiting your local library. You may also want to buzz on to these great websites for more information about mosquitoes:

- www.kidshealth.org/kid/ill_injure/aches/mosquito.html
- http://science.howstuffworks.com/mosquito.htm
- www.cdc.gov/ncidod/dvbid/westnile/prevention_info.htm
- http://whyfiles.org/016skeeter/index.html

This photographer is allowing a mosquito to bite his finger so he can take a picture of it.

Glossary

Note: Boldfaced words that are defined in the book may not appear in the glossary.

camouflage Markings or colorings that help an animal blend in with its surroundings

digest To break down food

exoskeleton The hard outer covering on an insect's body

insect An animal that has six legs, a pair of wings, and no backbone

insect repellent A spray or lotion with scents that confuse insects and make them stay away

hibernate To enter a state of deep sleep during cold months

organ A body part that does a specific job, such as pumping blood

saliva A liquid that is used to help break down food

sperm The reproductive fluid of a male animal

swarm marker A landmark around which male mosquitoes gather to attract females

vaccine A small dose of an infection, which prepares the body to protect itself in case of a serious infection

Index

1 2 3 4 5 6 7 8 9 0   Printed in the U.S.A.   3 2 1 0 9 8 7 6 5 4